Tossed To & Fro

Lisa Robinson Douglas

ROYSTON
Publishing

BK Royston Publishing
P. O. Box 4321
Jeffersonville, IN 47131
502-802-5385
http://www.bkroystonpublishing.com
bkroystonpublishing@gmail.com

© Copyright – 2019

All Rights Reserved. No part of this book may be reproduced, stored in a retrieval system, or transmitted by any means without the written permission of the author.

Cover Design: Gad – Elite Covers

ISBN-13: 978-1-951941-00-0

Printed in the United States of America

Dedication

To My Mother,

June Delores Robinson

Acknowledgements

Colossians 3:17 "Whatever you do, whether in word or deed, do it in the name of Jesus Christ, giving thanks to God and the father by him."

I first pondered with the thought of this write. I then prayed. After years of waiting I'm ever so thankful unto you my Lord for the birthing, hearing, preparing, blessing and now completing. I bow down unto you my Lord in TOTAL ADORATION. Praise will I forever speak and render unto you GOD. HALLELUJAH. AMEN

My parents James and June Robinson were so many of my firsts. From giving me life, prayer coverings, their teachings and encouragement influenced me and have made me who

I am today. Daddy may you rest on, in eternal peace, I love & miss you unmeasurably. Know that I'm fulfilling my promise to you of taking care of mommy. Most importantly you both were my first loves, teachers, friends, etc. Thankful unto God for giving me you.

To my first born, my son Adam Tavon Mckay. You have always been of a strong and determined character. I'm so thankful for your tenacity as it has encouraged me to push this write. Trust me when I say I've always been proud of you my love. The respect and mannerisms you gift out have been spoken of by many. This makes mommy so proud. I've seen time and time again your leadership ability. I CALL YOU CONQUERER. Love you infinitely my prince.

To my baby girl, my daughter Kiana Sheree Jackson. MY US ARMY SHERO. Thank you for your service my love. I CALL YOU LAUGHTER. As you have always been good for my soul. The memories we've created I revisit on a regular basis for I know they will make my heart smile. Your uniqueness & style makes me proud in knowing that you need no approval from man. You are mommy's sunshine. May your light shine on. I love you infinitely my princess.

My sisters Karen and Torri Robinson. We've shared more experiences than most. From the tight space of our childhood bedroom. We have matured enough to get through all of our differences today. I'm so grateful for all of the shares we've been through. The births of our children, our joys, our hardships and tears as well as the abundance of laughter. These memories will remain forever stored in my heart. As the baby girl I always wanted what you both had. I'm now thankful that your knowledge and teachings taught me the how to's of LIFE!

To the sisters of my first founded organization BABES (Blessed Always By Exceptional Sisters) Where do I start? From the initial invite extended, to the final group meeting, each of you demonstrated a desire of total commitment. The faithful dedication to succeed allowed BABES to be a positive force within the community. Without any barriers or reservations, we blessed so many. From the Multiple Sclerosis and Susan G Komen cure for cancer walks, to raising well over seven thousand dollars. From feeding the homeless in the community and adopting families for Christmas. Mouths were fed and I can hear the children's laughter. Thankful for our love and compassion for helping others allowed us to meet our goals. The invite stood then and will forever stand as you all play such a significant part of my life and growth. Each one of you gave so much, allowing us to grow and forever be bonded until this day. I love you ladies for that reason and so much more. Be on the lookout for Chapter two.

To all of my family members, my brothers my nephews, my nieces I love you all dearly. Shaniya thank you for all of the auntie-niece conversations you taught me how to reserve myself young lady. The walks we shared; they gave me encouragement sweetheart.

To my sidekick Faith thanks for always wanting to be by my side.

To my Mushienina, my niece Joi Robinson, I am so proud of the woman you have become. Your witty side reminds me of how important it is to let the little girl in me live! When I was at a low, we shared some text messages that taught me so much! How important it is to not fuel or feed my anger! Thank you love.

To the woman that encouraged, loved and cared enough. You ladies always made me feel like I mattered. From my heart to yours I love you all and I am so thankful you've shared in my journey. Barbara Hawkins (Bobbi) Joyce Hackley, Andrea Jackson (bug), Peggy Washington (shang shang), Chrystal Churchman (styles) Luv Berkley (sissy). There are many that have been a part of my life's walk. From a youthful woman to the matured woman I've grown to be. I don't take your involvement in my life lightly as you've played a significant role in my teachings and learnings. May the love of the Lord along with his grace and mercy directly shine over you. May his will direct you. May your walk with him and his wants for your life be plentiful, Blessings beloveds.

Table of Contents

Dedication	iii
Acknowledgements	v
Preface	xiii
Introduction	xxv
Before the Beginning	1
The Beginning	13
The Suffering	23
Peace in It All	37
Tossed Again and Peace After It All	49
Epilogue	67

Preface

As the chapters and verses are dropped in my spirit, the word melancholy comes forth in my thinking. Nostalgic feelings and memories of my childhood is what I believe taught me so much. Most definitely through the earlier part of my adulthood. Uncertainties of how I would face the next challenge as I continuously had been tossed to & fro. The momentums of Depression and Suppression were definitely the direction I always expected. Truth be told, in all I went through, I now know and believe I was being prepared as the Lord was doing a great work in me.

I've had many encounters with abuse. As an inquisitive teenage girl, I nearly experienced rape. I can still feel his fist hitting my face and the shot gun nozzle in mouth. These memories I've struggled to forget. Being called out of my name became a norm. Where ever there was lack I allowed negative decision making to overflow. Neglecting myself to please many was a huge mishap of mine. Disconnecting from reality nearly always resulted in how I dealt with most negative situations. Throughout my life I was wondering "why me" and where was my silver spoon! I eventually found my answers as my relationship with Christ evolved. "Why Not Me," for God is no respecter of persons. Now realizing all that I put my spiritual daddy through, the whippings he gave me can never compare to what Jesus had endured. Forgive me for my candidness, but I've learned there is another way to be and think. In all of it, my help cometh from the Lord "Abba God" the Great I Am.

You see, I've always presented with a personable personality. A leader by nature, talented for the most part, loving, caring, smart, beautiful as well as an all-around fun type of person.

Beneath the surface when the metaphor "chaos is a friend of mine" continually rang out. I now know why. For what was being birthed in me! I'm preparing my readers to walk in my nine and a half, sometimes ten shoes. No pity please. I'll accept the understanding while you're praising God as it all has worked out for the good. My experiences have resulted in completely encouraging this self-help write. From my writing to your reading, may my truths bring forth a great reward.

I wish I could call him a personal friend of mines, as he has certainly been of much encouragement to me.

I've never had the privilege of meeting Associate Pastor John Gray of Lakewood Church and his lovely wife Aventer. They are a power couple being led by Christ. If I may, on September 17, 2017 I was watching a televised sermon by Pastor Gray, I was then in a Tossing To and Fro season of my life. I had lost three very important men in my life. It was destined for me to hear this word in that moment. Never quenching nor compromising when the Holy spirit nudges me, I jumped up, ran and got a pen and some paper. I sat on my seats edge as the word of God was being ministered to me once again in my living room. A very familiar thing as mother and father would sit with me and we would watch so many television sermons being delivered. I've gotten completely off of the subject. forgive me y'all. Charge it to my head not my heart. Now, Pastor Gray was referencing The Book of 1st Samuel. The topic was of King David's battle with Goliath the giant. Yes, that oh so familiar text. It's referenced so often as a reflection to the lives of so many. The five Stones and the shepherd's bag. How many times have we all had to go into our bag and pull out stones to use against the enemy? This is why I could relate so earnestly.

My former Pastor Howard Butler used to crack my side when he would always say "keep on living." I now know what he meant and have become very familiar with the statement. Trust me when I tell you I became even the more eager in completing this write. For I knew it would be of encouragement to someone. For if only one would read it and receive all of what it was intended to do, its purpose would have been fulfilled. "The defeat has been beat" and "The Victory has been won."

The Lord most certainly can do ALL THINGS I know. He was allowing me to stay right in that moment. He was molding and preparing my steadfast and unmovable positioning. For the upcoming of my next tossing was near. I would come face to face with it and he was filling me with all the ammunition I would need. Just like the five stones he had given King David. The Lord has always prepared us with what we need in him. Only if discernment, to say the least would play a bigger part of our learning as we walk with him. Sometimes laying prostate in God is needed most for the hearing and receiving of his will for our lives. I've personally learned to be submissive to my Lord as this is the best walk, I've ever journeyed in. God has the control of all of my circumstance and situations. Whenever I thought I was in control with my big bad self, I wrecked it and now here comes the tossing, again! I felt like a boomerang that did a three sixty slapping my face ten times over. Now I'm sitting and waiting like the elephant in the room to be rescued. Only if I had learned early on how to put me aside in my mess, surrendering it all to God. Now, your to and fro tossings, may not be completely the same as mine. But God is no respecter of persons so He shall walk you through it. Do your work though. Faith without it is dead.

The actual day before I was talking to a friend of mines named Karen. We have shared many conversations regarding Gods goodness. It's ironic that we share so many similarities in life. From our relationship issues, birthdays being a day apart and love of the Lord, we have fellowshipped many days calling on the name of Jesus. Praying that he keeps us in his will. Now some folk that know me may say why is she spilling all of her personal business in this write. Let me clarify something to those that may need it. I've since come to learn that a healing only takes place when the truth is told. I'm quoting Gods words to me when he met me in my bathroom one night during MY DELIVERANCE! Growth only comes through release of all that has been holding you hostage. So, if a deliverance needs to take place, we must rid out selves of some stuff, you hear me!

I've learned how to meet defeat and that's head on. I'm far from perfection. With that being said, God doesn't expect my trying to be perfect. He works best in those who are willing to come openly. As a dead man/woman walking, meet God with all of your to and fro circumstances bowing down and submitting. It feels so good. Romans 4:17 This is the presence of him whom he believed God, who gives life to the dead. and calls the things that are not as though they were. Proverbs 3:5 Trust in the Lord with all your heart and lean not on your own understanding. Philippines 4:13 I can do all things through Christ whom strengthens me. I'm now walking a bountiful path in Christ which he promised. From today forward as a result of my walking in the Lords will for my life. He assures me that my being tossed to and fro depends solely on my How's. How to think, react, trust, give, receive, grow, etc. in Christ Jesus. As he is the author and the finisher of our faith.

Introduction

From being cursed out and stained from the many names I had been called. Gods AGAPE love rescued me. The sad part is when you believe all the negative things said to be true, the truth hurts. From not understanding how important unconditional love can be to your self-esteem building. The scars of not knowing such caused detriment to a healthy growth and wellbeing. From every belittling name I've been called it appeared to have line up with my physical flaws. I acknowledged the words as hurt and they took me to a broken place. Looking in the mirror from the eyes of a broken child my soul ached unwittingly. From seeing through my adult eyes, the truths I saw and recognized. Continual prayer for change was offered. These changes needed to manifest in order for healing and growth to come to life. I was overweight and depressed. This resulted from my lack of self-love and not knowing it. The cry baby in me was my pain and hurt speaking out. My tattle tailing as a whole was simply my cry for attention. Looking for someone to pacify me was simply not enough. Now realizing how to accept me through self-nurturing and discipline, the results are so positive and much more of a self-reward.

I knew it was near as change began to unfold. Seeing and feeling the desire many times over my life course was obvious. I would call on the Lord regularly but I couldn't reach him. Until this one particular day in October of 2003 when I was rescued. I had finally found what I had been missing and there was a thirsty desire to change. For in Christ Jesus I found peace and solitude. I had made a conscious decision to accept my Lord and Savior as my own. My life's detriments began to have meaning when they unfolded. For I would be in and out of season knowing that my savior lives and would be with me through it all. The desire and my wanting to change began to shake me up when I stepped out of God's will. I wanting to do right and better is where It landed me, through it all. I now know why the lord placed this title on my heart and mind. Let the tossing begin. Literally I knew there would be things I would come up against. I knew who I was and who God was to me. The ability he gave for us to be able to do all things through him was magnified tenfold in my thought process. My strengths became stronger and my weaknesses easier to deal with. The tossing to and fro became understandable as it hadn't been up to this point. Now, with the pen hitting the paper the explaining begins. It was then over a decade ago when the unrevealing truth of God's promises came to me. It looked me in the face. I had met the Great I Am. I must say the things that were missing from my life, God's presence alone fulfilled in me. Not being accepted by some he was always welcoming. The yearning for love and his fulfilling keeps me in a safe place. Whether at my lowest or my highest I know who to call upon. And his praise shall continuously be in my mouth. Amen truth!

Chapter 1
BEFORE THE BEGINNING

Being the youngest of five children consisting of two brothers and two sisters, with a mom and dad present, I was thankful. Always feeling that extra sense of being provided for. My parents worked hard and provided for us responsibly. Mother was the disciplinarian, as dad was the gentle giant with the stern stature. He was the run to guy when moms' feathers were ruffled. Shoot, I can remember getting slapped in the face with a wet dishrag or the back of mom's hand many a days. Momma didn't play nor take no mess. OUCH. I know some can relate. I always felt something was absent from what appeared to be right to many. I can vaguely remember some of the happy times. I question myself in why it's so easy to remember the sad times. It's crazy how life's focuses are more on the bad than the good times. What I used to hold most dear to me were the sad memories as they without regard would playback in my memory many nights. As children, we were cursed out more than showered with expressions of love. It's so sad I have no recollection of being told as a child "I love you." The words my mommy dearest once spewed out to me was that 'I was one that she should have aborted' rang over and over in my ear disrupting my love for self! My mommy gave it to us raw. No filter whatsoever. She didn't care who didn't like it either. Well, it was a behavior she learned as her mother gave off the same. Mommy demanded respect in the same scenario also. Like "yes ma'am" and you better not suck your teeth, nor roll your eyes, or you got it. You know that 'do as I say not as I do' mentality. Generational behaviors and curses were carried down, alive and present. Everybody was doing and screwing everybody. Believing we (the children) didn't know or wouldn't remember. Yet and still expecting and demanding the highest of respect and standards from us. Apparently, forgetting the behaviors they demonstrated were taught and learned. Don't act surprised that we all carry the curses of our ancestors and parents. Some will admit and break the curse, others submit to and carry the curse. I gave up that ghost when my parenting began.

Now in my life before the beginning, childhood dinners were most likely eaten alone than shared together around the family table.

I'm thankful to the least that a meal was provided every night. Not once can I remember not having food of some sort to eat. Saturdays were for cereal, cartoons and cleaning. Sundays meant mommy was in the kitchen singing gospel songs preparing us for church with no exception of not going. Something was still absent from the equation in my reflect. Now, what I do remember was stringing popcorn on Christmas eves in the Robinson household. Along with the big breakfasts mom prepared on most Sundays. Lord yes, and those homemade cakes from scratch. Me and my sisters fussing over the stirring spoon and bowl dripping with cake mix. Y'all know what I'm talking about. Fun times on the block with the neighborhood kids. From the Rons, Veronicas, Verinas, Bruce Keiths and Poppies of your neighborhoods.

Playing run catch and kiss still make my inner child tingling with warmth as those days were good. Thank you, Hancock street crew. Johnny on the pony and skelly were the popular ones with the boys. But Lordy, when the girls came out to play, run catch & kiss and spin the bottle was fire. Trying to be grown doing grown folk stuff when we were still dripping wet behind the ears. The memories of the good old days and that nostalgic feeling leaves me smiling.

My sisters Torri and Karen shared in doing sibling things with me when we were younglings. As we grew up, the arguing, fussing and many times fighting became the normal. Vague memories of us sharing loving times for the life of me I can't pull out. I wish I did have more memories of us bonding. Was it ever really there that I questioned myself?

My adult, all grown up inner mind continuously reflects on the lack thereof. The what if's and what of's simply don't hold dear to me now. In my adult all grown up self, I vowed to give more love now.

As a teenager, I was focused more on seeking attention from my home girls and homeboys. The streets and what it taught me I think did well. No sense of staying in my mess as I've grown from my regrets. My friends and I spent so much time together that we played a huge part in the lessons we learned and made it through. We watched one another grow up and into experiencing our first loves and becoming mothers and fathers. Most of my girlfriends and I shared in common of being the baby of the family. So, our experiences of being thrown away by our older siblings resulted in sharing the feelings of not being wanted. I'm so thankful in knowing my childhood. Now, my adult friends have done well in spite of all the life's challenges. I'm honored in saying we all still share in bonded friendships even though we are many miles apart.

As I grew into a young woman approaching the tender age of twenty, I met the man who would three years later become my baby daddy. That characteristic "my Baby Daddy" suits this man to the tee. To say the least, as he has fathered seventeen different children to seventeen different women. I take complete credit to my ignorance in knowing I should have known better. I was much younger than him as he was fifteen years my senior. His lifestyle attracted me in my immatureness and

I wanted to get just what I got. He was a drug dealer and a ladies' man. Seven years I dealt with mess I wasn't matured enough to handle nor was I mentally equipped with the outcome of what would become. There was so much absence of good morale that his respect for me kept me hurting. I wasn't mentally capable of knowing my worth as a person or woman, to realize what I needed he wasn't offering. I settled for what felt good and the materialistic gain in the situation. All the getting of what I got couldn't compare to all I needed. Having a "JAFAKEMAN," oops I'm sorry I shouldn't have said that. My intention was never to discredit a race or person. But, having a drug dealing Jamaican man back then was the phase and hype thing to do. Particularly because my neighborhood was booming with Jamaican drug dealers back then. He gave me everything

I wanted that money could buy. Eventually the buying of things was not enough. I wanted more than I would ever get. The mist of what I got was plenty of heartaches. Confrontations from other woman along with physical altercations as we all wanted what we would never have. It took me physically slitting his wrist open with a switch blade and cutting all four of his tires before realizing I just couldn't anymore. It was a 'save myself' type of relationship as the 'he and I' ship was sinking before leaving the dock. I was completely worn out from the seesaw effects of the ups and downs from the hurt before my son reached the tender age of seven months old. The most hurtful memory I have of the time shared was catching my baby daddy with another woman and their newborn infant. My prince (son) was seven months at the time.

That was the revelation I needed in knowing this negro ain't got no change in him. The hurt I endured from this entire ordeal was enough to make me pack a bag and roll out. I put my baby on my hip, copped a greyhound bus from Penn Station 42nd Street in New York and rolled out. Orange County Virginia is where we wound up. At this point, the parenting of my son became my heart's desire. There was no room for error. Getting it right was the only option. He was my focus and my goal. Envisioning a future of peace, happiness most importantly was the need. I vowed to instill all the love my heart carried into my child.

    I landed a job and slept on a family member's floor until I could do better. I remember the phone call I received from my mother's sister (Aunt Jean), rest her soul. She said, Baby, come live with me, you and your son." That's just what I did. I packed my baby boy up, heel and toe, and off we went.

After several years of hurt and feeling de humanized, my passion for relationships subsided and my focus become more on parenting. The love of my son opened a newness in me. The feeling that I had been missing for so long. Never to discredit or take away from my parents or any of my family members, I've since learned that everyone is not capable of giving everyone what they need. Not everyone requires or wants to be loved. Fortunately, I'm one of those that do. I know that Love alone is such a reward in itself that I wouldn't want it any other way. "For God so loved this world that he gave his only begotten son that whosoever believe in him shall have everlasting life." John 3: 16. In this earth, relying on the good news in all of this, is the reward of love and respect, kindness, peace, joy and so much more of life. Goodness only makes life that much better.

Chapter 2
THE BEGINNING

My first born, my love, my heartbeat, my son, entered the world on January 10th 1987. He was perfect in my eyes. My heart filled with joy. He made a grand entrance as that of a lion wanting to control the situation. He was delivered of a cesarean due to the complications of being breech. Wanting to be in control even upon birth, a valor my son has displayed ever since. I knew I had to woman up in that very moment and my mothering duties would be of great reward. Without question, it was the joy of birthing my prince and this new move would bring great fulfillment to my life.

My son would soon be approaching

toddler age when I met a man. Unfortunately, in my immatureness, the feeling of liking this man was what mattered most to me. The fact remained that he was my cousin's 'live in lover' didn't matter. The attraction I can now admit to was not the focal point as to why I hooked up with him. My old behaviors tossed me right back to what I was running from. Yes, the drug dealing and materialistic attributes of what he was offering was the pattern to my selfless love. No excuses only truths are what I must admit. I had another date with Satan and his tactics to fulfill my flesh. This scenario was playing out so poorly disrupting my family. Generational curses were intertwined and being carried out through myself and other family members. No one had the nerve to stand up to this mess and fight the temptations of fulfilling the flesh. I've since then matured enough to apologize with most regard to my cousin. We fought against the ethics of good, He and I married despite my mother's wishes. She did tell me she would never give us her blessings. So, cursed we were. In spite of postponing the marriage two times, we later married before the justice of the peace then had a small reception at my parent's home.

My relationship with this man consisted of similarities that were all too familiar with past relationships. What was I doing wrong was the question I continued to ask myself? Not realizing then that two broken people could never complete one another. We struggled from day to day with even the likes of each other's presence. From his insecurities to my not trusting him played a huge part in the failed relationship. The stimulating attraction had died down sooner than later. I had nothing to keep me motivated on making us work. At this point, wanting a baby from this man appeared to be a good idea. Sound crazy right? After two years, I gave birth to a beautiful baby girl on August 1st, 1990. She brought so much joy to my life as I knew she would love me and I her. My husband and I worked hard enough to put everything else aside, including our feelings for one another. From living with his aunt and uncle to moving in with my parents, I felt lack in so many areas. When my baby girl turned two, I remember finally moving into an apartment. Starting out was the hardest. We didn't have much. I remember having many hand me downs that were so appreciated at the time. We struggled with trying to parent and satisfy each other's desires. We just felt so wrong. I was being accused of cheating when the thought of it never crossed my mind. The repetition of being called a fat 'you know what,' became too familiar. Respect didn't live at my address during those days. Now being so understanding of how Karma works, I'm at peace. Well time passed and unhappy feelings grew us further apart. We co-existed for the sake of marriage and parenting. I can remember playing the dozens one day. It got intense as name calling and teasing usually does. If I direct my memory long and hard enough, I can still feel his hands around my neck. My worst days were here, and now decisions would have to be made. From bailing my husband out of jail on more than one occasion resulting from his drunk driving to his cheating on me and admitting it, I felt violated, unloved and unappreciated. One night as we lay in bed asleep, he sat up on his side of the bed. I asked with concern, "What's wrong?" What my ears would hear in that moment would never line up with what my heart could take. My husband asked me how could my son look so much like his grandfather? It still brings tears to my eyes. The insinuation that I had borne my son as a result of sleeping with my father would be the last insult to my intelligence. For the reasons of keeping my sanity, I knew something needed to be done immediately. The next day I packed my children up and left my residence. I refuse to call it my home. As I now know, a home should be filled with love and never bring so much hurt. The reasoning behind my husband's accusations would later come from his warped thoughts. The fact of him learning that I had a different biological father than my siblings. Unfortunately for him, he would take something of such sentiment to me and use it against me. In my deepest thoughts of sharing this secret with him, never crossed my mind of the hurt it would later bring. Shoot, I had learned of this when my daughter was only three months old. Having to live with this hidden secret deep in my soul held me captive. For the sake of not interrupting the peace in my family, being sworn to secrecy would be a ghost burden I would have to carry. Lord knows I wouldn't dare for the sake of salvaging my happiness, reveal it. Pressing on was my attempt, but in reality, being tossed to and fro was the norm. I had been tossed again. This pattern of unhappiness would later bring me to a place where I would have to bow down. I couldn't for the life of me grip what feeling complete would look like. I knew no other way then to brush it off and pull up my big girl panties (literally). Trying again to make better choices that would reward my life and family. I did just that at this point. I stayed away from the home long enough to gain my sanity back as my husband's words ripped through me and needed mending. Only time and the Lord would heal. Unfortunately, I was not in relationship with him then, God I mean.

I took on a relationship with the woman that managed the apartment complex I lived in. I would later return home and began to have a very close relationship and friendship with her. I would later find out why she took me under her wing. She had the maintenance department to change the locks on the apartment. My husband left after believing he would be responsible for paying the rent and bills. I came back to an apartment and I created it into a home. I met another person that took on the role of a big sister. She was a confident and dear friend. We bonded and shared so many great times that I would forever hold dear to me as Joyce Hackley. Her old soul gave unto the emptiness of teachings I needed. As she taught me so much, we shared over fifteen years of friendship. Our children grew, learned and were taught together.

Chapter 3
THE SUFFERING

One of the hardest things I ever had to deal with was facing it, learning from it and dealing with my truths. My recollection of it all is very clear. I contemplated and tossed with how to vaguely write this chapter. After praying and asking the Lord how to, his instruction was that everything is not for everyone's ears to hear. So, he gave me what was needed to be shared. I was in my mid-twenties. As a matter of fact, I can remember the day, the hour and the minute down to the second. This very moment has played over and over again time after time over the years. My baby girl was two months old when someone dear to me shared a hidden family secret with me that would forever change my life. The reveal affected me to the core: my outlook on people, my circumstances, my life and mainly my HEART. My trust for people had been damaged. It even resulted in my physical health diminishing as I hid from that secret and suffered from depression. Had to seek medical attention resulting in me taking prescribed medication for it. As my pen reaches the paper in completing this chapter, I still struggle forcing the tears back. It was a warm day as summer was near its end. I toiled back and forth with how to present my mother with this question I had two days earlier learned of. I called her to my bedroom after crying with the fear of not knowing how to. It took every fiber of my being to ask. "Mother, do I have a different father than my sisters and brother." Already knowing that my mother's oldest of the five children, one son, was born to her first marriage. The hardest attempt to making light of such a serious question was impossible. I just blurted it out! I remember saying, "Mother, if I'm wrong, please forgive me." Nonetheless, I was unprepared for the life changing impact her answer would have on me. She replied, "I'm not gonna discuss this right now." In that very moment, I felt my heart stop. I knew whose I wasn't and also whose I was. Remember that gentleman I spoke of in chapter 2, "The Beginning." Yes him, that was the man that fathered me. Shortly after that, I had the opportunity of being introduced to him as his daughter. My father and I stood face to face. The stench of alcohol mixed with old spice annoyed my nostrils, amongst other things. His repeated attempts to make me feel better only brought hurt. "I'm sorry, Baby.

You were made out of love" rang out over and over and over again. I wasn't seeking reasoning behind him and my mother's actions. The hurt needed to dissolve within me solely not of either of their deeds. Nor would I play God by judging the two responsible for my DNA. I was strong enough to understand how the act took place and weak enough in my twenty-five-year-old self to absorb it. Now, the how to handle it and the effects this would have over me was the struggle. I gained clarity in the physical and visible attributes as so many people had questioned my light skinned complexion verses my siblings. I was certainly my father's daughter and everyone knew it and could see it. He could have never been denied that. So, why me? Why had they waited so long was the question? A question that the answer simply was not enough. "We didn't know how you would handle it!" By now, my husband was aware of the situation. He would attempt in using this against me in the future. I never thought that my informing him would bring me more pain than less. As you will read, it was the furthest thing from my thoughts.

Over the next couple of months, I had the pleasure of spending lots of time with Mr. Herbert Johnson (Butch). I learned so much about him, me and who I was as a result of him. He shared stories with me about my grandparents. He told me that his father was a German man that owned lots of land and property in West Virginia. He shared of his mother's position as a house maid to his father. My heart dropped when he told me his mother had been raped several times by his father (her master) resulting in his being born. He informed me of all the siblings I had and their localities. He was such a pleasure to be around. Mr. Johnson continuously reminded me over and over again of being created in love. It was as if he could sense the need of telling me what I've for so long felt to be missing. In his presence alone, the reassurance of a love that I'd been missing came to life.

It was so crazy that he and my daddy shared so much in character. Two good looking men of strong stature. Humility and integrity were top priority playing a big role in characters. Needless to say, from this moment forward, these two men would play a crucial role in the lives of me and my children. The hurt was subsiding knowing that I had two men in my life that I could call 'Dad.' I felt honored that this situation was turning out for my good.

Did I mention I had been sworn to secrecy? Yes, the task of keeping this hidden from my family as requested of my mom and Mr. Johnson reigned heavy on my heart. I wrestled with the thought of this demand forever. The result of this tossed me right back in a state of depression. How dare them in their infidelities make their sin for me to bare? I gave my word to keep their secret hidden. Honestly, I tried. Years past, my children grew up and it became impossible to contain.as Mr. Johnson made more frequent trips from his home in Washington DC to visit me and his grandchildren.

Years passed and for lack of better words my keeping my sanity was pertinent. I sat my children down and had a family meeting with them. I explained in depth according to their age level what I felt would be appropriate in explaining. My children were inquisitive and always asking who he was. I told them that the man I thought to be my father was not, but that he raised me as his own. The hurt they let off feeling as if grandpapa was no longer their grandpapa saddened me so. I assured them that grandpapa would always be their grandpapa. I told them that I found out through a family friend and no one knew that I knew. I swore them to secrecy. You see how this general curse played out continuing to haunt my family.

The one person that I confided in, as spouses should, was the very person to slap me in the face with this secret down the road. My husband at the time later twisted the thought of knowing that the man that raised me as his daughter was not my biological father. His demented thoughts. His accusations of how could my son look so much like his grandfather when he was not biologically his, raged anger in me. His opinion of me having no integrity warranted the divorce. Shame on him and his twisted thoughts of me being that low as a woman, a daughter and a person. We all know that man/woman is not like god and will let you down. Well his synopsis of my character embarrassed me. His hidden agendas and infidelities led him to believe that I was of such a low standard. When in all truth, how could my learning of such cause so much pain and separation within my family? How many of us know that the truth hurts so many of us as an outcome to all of this.

Generational curses, being in bondage, strongholds, lies, etc. All of these horrible behaviors are not truths. My heart needed to set free. A deliverance needed to take place, as I was living the lie that was in me. Secretly lies, secrets and more lies. The main reason behind this writing is to make known the detriment of living a lie and harboring untruths and the results that will follow. Fast forwarding to maybe ten years down the road. My children and I had spent many years getting to know my biological dad, brother and sisters. We visited them on occasion and he visited my home many times always coming with gifts to express his love and loss time. I felt honored as he was a joy to be around. He reminded me on each visit of the love he had for me. He apologized for not being in my life. He cried, I cried and we cried together. "What have I done?" he would say? Repeatedly saying, "You are my love child." I forgave him but the hurt would take more than words to dissolve. As this was buried down deep in my soul. Only God could repair me in my broken places.

Time stopped as my dad was approaching his mid-eighties. Traveling from Washington DC to VA became a safety issue and became less. Then the telephone calls stopped. I then found myself tossed back in time to where I was that day, I confronted my mother. I no longer had that someone to love me unconditionally. The memories of our hugs, laughs, smiles and cries began to pop up in my thoughts. Nights of crying longing for the smell of his alcohol breath and old spice I would have given anything for. Praying and asking God, why? Then the realization of him never coming back taunted me and I became bitter. Bitter in the life that I had but the circumstances I didn't create. God why?

My dad's health took a turn for the worse. I received a phone call that he was in John Hopkins Hospital in Washington, DC. He had fallen and broke his hip. Infection set in and he was being cared for. I was casted out and not allowed to visit for fear of the secret coming out. He was later released and sent home. His wife and children weren't made aware of me. I was the secret. I wanted to call to hear his voice but I couldn't. My heart ached immensely. My dad died on January 10, 2016 (my son's birthday). I was not allowed to attend his funeral. The love he extended to me after meeting and getting to know him was a lifetime worth. I will forever treasure it. I love and miss you Mr. Herbert Johnson (Butch). The man that I grew to know as my daddy.

CHAPTER 4
PEACE IN IT ALL

This writing was birthed in me nearly fifteen years ago. Seven years later, I began to write down my thoughts and feelings concerning it. The last four years, it began to come to life. The awakening of it began as a challenge and appeared very difficult. It was 2005, the year my prince was graduating high school. I can still see the smile on his face as he walked head held high across that stage. On the ride home from the graduation ceremony, he screamed out the window of our moving vehicle, "No more school for me, I'm done." It was in that moment that I realized he had become a man graduating school. I still had my princess to graduate and then I would be alone.

Shortly after that, almost two weeks later, I received a telephone call that would forever change my life and thoughts of being alone. A telephone call requesting my hand in marriage. This was an old flame. A man I had dated in the past. He was calling me from Florida. His request came as a surprise to me as we had only dated twice. He told me he loved me and could not stop thinking of me and hoped that one day I would honor his wish in becoming his wife and marrying him. I received a second phone call three weeks later. He would be arriving in Virginia shortly. He was traveling by a rental car and asked if I would pick him up. I was excited by the phone call as the two dates were memorable and seeing him again would be very nice. The thought of the request of my hand in marriage made it all the easier too.

We were two different people sharing nothing in common I must admit as our conversation revealed. Desperation for love and a relationship I must say was my reasoning to ignore what I was feeling. What I mean is that, we were so excited about our outer selves that we never got familiar with one another's heart. We both were longing for something hopeful and that we had what each other needed. We both longed for internal love. He had lost his dad at 18 years old and was in search of himself. I was seeking love as I never really knew it. I always dreamt of my prince charming coming into existence to sweep me off of my feet. His jumping off the pages of a Cinderella book would be just right. How many of you all know that didn't happen? The bruises and ruins of the lack of love, disrespect, immaturity was so heavy it weighed us down. From his phone being locked as if he was hiding something kept me having trust issues with this man. I remember moving him in because of the request without even discussing it. Desperate, I was shall I say. I don't need any cosigners. I can vouge for myself. We were attracted to one another with good intentions. Sad to say, intentions weren't enough to bring us where we needed to go.

He moved in with me and we forced love upon one another for four years. We then had an absolutely beautiful wedding. A marriage it was not. He would never admit it for the sake of his pride, but we were broken in many pieces. In spirit, in love, in growth and most importantly our relationship. Growth was not in it. I always felt I was the better person as his infidelities led him to cheating and getting caught. Out of the several times I was aware of, his cheating had become obvious. The final time, he was caught in the act with a woman at the hotel. Yeah, she called me the day before to tell me he was cheating on her with another woman they worked with. Yes, she was a hot mess thinking she was doing me a favor. As I sat with her in her car, she filled me with what they shared on many occasions. Her cell phone rang as she prepared me knowing he would be on his work break calling soon. She smiled as he told her how and what he wanted to do to her. I pretended it didn't bother me just to bate her in, feeling like a fool and acting like one as well. All the long, I would never ever handle a situation as such in my present state. I forgave him and stayed once again. I would have never believed it would be part of my healing and story. Some stuff was brewing in me that needed to transpire. I would be made whole eventually. Many times, I wanted to get out as I'm sure he did also. As matter of fact, I separated from the marriage two times. He was asked to leave two times as well. The coming back was the easy part. I needed to stay until the instructions were given. You see when you are not equipped and given instruction, you are headed for destruction. I once heard someone say, "You shouldn't try to diminish your brains brilliance but rather bolster your soul's strength." This statement was an awakening in me as I knew better mentally and spiritually. The Holy Spirit lives within us, our souls. All of us. My spirit man had told me not to take this walk two times. Pleasing my flesh was most important to me, so the consequences I had to endure. The great thing about my Lord is that he forgives, restores and gives you all of what you need to continue this walk with him.

Tired became the norm for me. Peace within I did not have. Depression consumed me. My mental, my physical and my spiritual selves were being tossed around. I couldn't hold my head up and barely present a smile. Deep inside, I had known of the Lord prevailing as I had seen it many times before. I needed him now! Many of nights, I cried out to him. I was tired of me so I just knew God was tired of me too. My decision to stay and the thought of it tortured me and all I thought I was. I stayed in my relationship with hopes of it mending itself even though I knew we had to put in the work. That's not how life goes as we settle most times for the sake of saying I have a man let alone I have a husband.

It took nearly four years of unhappiness in the highest to hear from the Lord. I'm sure it was the works of the Lord and none of my own. I was at my most bitterness stage when my soul opened up. I remember pulling up in my driveway crying in the car. I knew putting my key in the door and going inside all too familiar. No pleasant conversations between us made us being in each other's presence intolerable. The conversation we did share that last evening together was violent and harsh. I just wanted to rest.

It all began when I decided to lay down after arguing. 'Peace be still' kept rising out in my ears. I put my earphones on as I was listening to some gospel as I did regularly. All of a sudden, I got extremely hot. I had no idea what was going on. I got up and went to the bathroom. I knelt down as I started to vomit. I then felt the presence of the Holy Spirit. When I tell you, his presence was wonderfully real even though I was physically feeling sick. I could feel the spirit moving in me beginning at my feet working up my body. I kept saying to myself, "Lord what is happening to me?" I was crying uncontrollably as I felt God's presence moving. When the Holy Spirit began to move, I knew in that moment that this was not a physical ailment. This was the second time for me having an experience like such. Except this time a purging was taking place. I needed to be rid of some stuff you hear me. My Lord, my lord, I needed this right now. I got up from my bathroom floor having the feeling of an outer body experience. I found my way back to my bed.

The Lord began talking to me. I can close my eyes and hear his voice right now. He said, "Have Teri and Mother Ora cover you." I replied, "Lord What?" He said, "Have Teri and Mother Ora cover you." I thought I knew why he was telling me this, but it was much deeper than my thoughts. It would all come together later. He then said, "Everything is not for everyone to hear." I immediately turned to my husband saying, "The lord is talking to me." His response was, "Shut the hell up! God ain't telling you nothing." I was so disgusted by his response that I laid back down and put my earphones back on. In that moment the Lord said, "Didn't I just tell you that? I tried immensely to control my crying and listen to the instruction. The Lord then said, "Move now..." This was the answer I had been praying for many years. I was so hopeful my marriage would change without any work being put in. I was certain my husband would become the man I wanted him to become. It was too late. I got my instructions after failing the test over and over again. I'll never claim to have been a perfect wife, but I was a good wife. I needed the Lord to help me do better for myself. I knew at that point the change had to be manifested. I cried I believe until I fell asleep that night. A night I will never forget. The presence of the Lord was real, and I'm so blessed in knowing he cares enough to step in when we feel we can't go any further. Who knows, the end result may have been detrimental. To God Be The Glory.

Chapter 5
Tossed Again and Peace After It All

I left my sorrow, hurt, pain, bitterness and husband behind. I hadn't prepared myself as it came like a thief in the night. It was nothing but the will of God. After hearing the spirit say, "move now," my prayers of staying or leaving my marriage had been answered. I hold no ill will. I just knew obedience was crucial for my growth. I had been ignorant for too long. I already had a bag packed, so when the Lord woke me up, I was out the door. Me, my overnight bag and new beginnings. I felt a sense of peace in my spirit. It needed to be protected. So here I was. Tossed right back in a place that I had become too familiar with. But this time I was determined to cancel out the feelings of loneliness with redirection. It was perfectly ok to take a different approach to managing my miserableness. Realizing I had to depend on the Lord for complete self-healing. I was willing and ready to find peace, growth and happiness within me, right now this time around. Do y'all know that many people struggle with being alone? Sad to say some end results have been fatal due to suicide for many. I'm so thankful. I simply had to minimize myself letting negative thoughts go. Now recognizing for myself. Identifying my inner strength enough to handle these thoughts and situations.

As the days turned into months, my focus on being a full-time caretaker of my parents is where life has taken me. Mother had been dealing with health issues resulting from a heart attack, six strokes, four bleeding ulcers, feeding tubs and so much more. Her health began declining around December 2015. My family had been dealing with "STUFF" for a while now. I watched my dad's health decline over the months. Dad first suffered and aneurysm in 2011 and had to learn life skills all over again. He was 87 years old and I felt that he was tired. I remembered the phone call that we received to come in to meet with his doctor. That was the worst. It was unexpected. His doctor informed us of dad's kidneys completely shutting down. The iodine dye used for imaging had caused many complications from a recent surgery. Daddy looked at me with a look of desperation in that moment. Then he shrugged his shoulders in sorrow looking pitiful. After the doctor informed us of the possibility of no more than six months to live, I dropped my head and I was so sorry because I didn't know what to say. I didn't know how to comfort him. Hospice was the suggested referrals. The ride home was filled with a thick silence that could only be cut by the sharp butcher's knife.

Dad suffered in his last days as his conditions took everything from him. His feebleness made him totally dependent on someone for complete care. This duty became our way with gratitude for our KING. He hadn't eaten anything in nearly seven days. Medications for pain were being pumped in and we weren't getting nothing in return. I tried my best to remain strong in this situation as my vow to be my parent's caretaker was so important to me. We did all we could to make daddy comfortable. I remember our church choir coming to sing to daddy as he loved hearing them sing. Kyra sang "Give me you," as this was a song he loved. Our Pastor Ronald Johnson (bless him) came to be with dad and this blessed his soul. During my son's visit with his granddaddy. I'm certain this brought joy to dad as Tavon held daddy's hand caressing him the entire visit. Not leaving his bedside. I remember my sister Karen feeding dad a teaspoon of peach juice. The old man loved him some peaches. Something so minimal bringing so much pleasure and having such meaning. It was nearly two weeks from the doctor's appointment that dad went home to be with the Lord. August 3, 2017 approximately 3:30 a.m. would forever change the lives of the Robinson family.

The evening leading to that night was

surreal. We had been shopping earlier that day. My sister Karen, my daughter Kiana Jackson and my niece Joi Robinson. Torri stayed with mother and daddy. After coming home, it was as if the Lord touched everyone in the house with a finger of sleep. This was so unusual as we were night owls. We would stay up laughing, talking, watching TV or simply hanging out. Not his night. We packed in bed like sardines at 10 p.m. Sleep had taken over. I can remember Joi waking me up after 3 a.m. with the news. She had heard mother wondering about down the hallway looking for dad. In disbelieve as to how he got out of bed in his weakness is still crazy. The Lord carried him to the bathroom where he would lay down and never get back up again. The suffering is over. The eternal peace of being with the Lord, his parents, his brothers and sisters must have calmed our thoughts. The family greeting him brought a smile to my face. I'm certainly no one's judge but I'm sure the Lord met daddy saying "welcome home thou good and faithful servant," you were a man of such great character. A provider to your family. Integrity was your way of life. I'm so lost without you. Daddy I am so thankful for all of our talks and your teachings. Losing you continues to hurt everyday but I'm certain you wouldn't want anything to hinder my growth. There had been many nights of loneliness I would be up against only prayer and faith would keep me. I'm here. I've always known that grace and mercy would sustain me. I'm satisfied with all of my learning. They say that experience is the best teacher. I say that the Lord is. The word shall henceforth be my teacher preparing me for all of life's lessons. If we just be the student that God would have us to be.

When God was purging me that day class was held in my bathroom. I had no knowledge of the prerequisites to the situation. The purging had to manifest as the Holy Spirit needed to rid me of some mess. Similar to a cleansing we take in the physical form. The instruction came next. The Lord told me to have Terri and mother Ora cover me. I knew not why at that time. But since then I've learned. Teri would be my prayer sister and warrior. As a woman of God, she cried and prayed with me until the assignment was fulfilled. I would take her kind words, prayers and teachings with me on this journey. Also, this journey would be a study guide and a cheat sheet. Mother Ora would be my personal disciplinarian. She would also hold me dear to her heart. She taught me that regardless to what I was going through to never let go of the Lord's hand. She continuously protected my mental faculties as she kept pouring into me. My heart was satisfied many times after visiting or talking with her. I'm thankful for many but more thankful for these people that God brought into my life at that time. The Lord will always have a ram in the bush. Now the essay would be the challenge as I had to do the work for myself. Nobody but me. Lord I need you now. It took a lot of brainstorming and preparing for this test. The lessons needed to be applied to this life's essay. I had to remember all of the prayers, side notes and lessons as the tests would come daily. Pop quizzes, exams, essays, finals shoot all kinds of test.

Life became easier each day. I was smiling again. The loss of my home and my husband hurt. But when the thought came in, I erased it. I learned to lean on the Lord and not my own understanding. Coming from a place of having my own home to having a single in my parent's home weighed in on my independence you know. Especially when I went into my room at night and closed the door. To say the MOST, I had to go through what I needed to in order for this write's manifestation. I'm so thankful.

Moving forward happier times and brighter days were ahead. The sun appeared to be shining more frequently. My gratitude through prayer became more and more. Reestablishing my relationship with God kept me. No matter how big or bad I thought I was

I needed him with me every second of each day. Now we all know that life is going to give us uncomfortable situations we must deal with. If it was not for his grace and mercy we would be lost. I try to apply the Lord and His love for me in my life daily as it is essential to stay in a PEACEFUL place. Like when my brother passed six months following my daddy's death. My brother was a treasure and I'm so pleased with knowing that he had that Lord in his life. That old ugly cancer snuck in like the thief it is. Peewee lived a full life. He truly enjoyed life each day. He was a hard worker and loved nice things. He loved to party laugh and have a good time. He reached for the stars and shot for the moon on a regular as he would say. I'm so thankful for his wife Rosita, my sister in law. Thankful that she knows the Lord for herself. Yes, she is faithful and knows the

Lord. As she was a dedicated wife committed to making sure he was comfortable. I'm so blessed that Peewee's daughter Deedee stayed faithful in being by his bedside and loving on him. So, this was another heart wrenching thing we had to deal with. But, with the Lord all things are possible. Earth has no sorrow that heaven cannot heal. God's comfort kept us in knowing there was no more suffering for daddy and Peewee. Missing the both of them with each passing day, but forever keep their memory in our hearts.

Getting through loss was difficult but it became easier. Life went on to the next chapter, next challenge. I had at this point been my mother's caretake for well over three years. The difficulty in this was her Medicaid had been cut her off. That meant they would no longer pay me for her care. My income was gone. First of all, let me say this, my mother would have been taken care of regardless. But how would I manage financially. Here we go again. PRAY, PRAY AND PRAY SOME MORE. Faith without works is dead. What do I do? I can't leave mom to go back to work. My health issues increased plummeting as my stress levels heightened. I was seeing my doctor more frequently with some high blood pressure, anxiety and depression. Mood swings on fleek and being called bipolar. Being put on depression medications was not where I needed or wanted to be. My family would suffer. As I would suppress my thoughts and feelings every day. Crying and having a pity party with myself every day. NOT BEING TOSSED BACKWARDS BUT BEING THROWN. I was in a place of loneliness again. I began to point the finger at family members. Their absence made me resent them. Hurtful things were said to and about them. Their presence made it nearly impossible for me to accompany. I had reached the level of not wanting to get up each day and out of bed. It became incredibly hard to provide the necessary care for my mother as well as myself. Well this too shall pass.

    I held on to God's never changing hand. The memory I had of his greatness needed to be revived. The mustard seed faith that dwelt in me would pull me from this dark place. The Lord has never failed me yet. Well, as I held on each day a spark of brightness would light up. His light began to shine within. I decided to walk most week day mornings. Some Sundays before church service also. This would not only be healthy for me physically but mentally as well. Let me tell you what it did for me spiritually. It gave me the opportunity to meet the sun each day. I prayed aloud each day during my walking. I would literally feel the Lord's presence with me. Many mornings I released my cries as I thanked the Lord for forgiving me. I was being refilled. The Lord was giving me so much more. Feeling of accomplishment set in as I was doing this on my own. I became thirsty, wanting more. Not only for more of the Lord's presence during my morning walks but it became visible and what woman doesn't love compliments. I was losing weight gaining confidence. The peace within me was growing. I didn't forget to say I stopped attending church regularly I wasn't ready to say it. Thank you, Lord, for the snatchback.

As a matter of fact, it was nearly six months. God never turning His back on me as I did Him. I'm forever thankful God is not like man. Many months passed and my confidence was on high. After months of neglecting myself, things began to turn around. Church became the norm again. I decided that I would never turn my back on His greatness ever again. As long as I can do all things through Him, I would be strengthened and praise his name. I felt I needed to pick back up on some of the goals I once dreamt of for myself. And here I am. Totally cognizant of who I've become. The Lord let me go through it to bring me to it. All kind of ideas were being birthed in me. Some old, some new. I wanted the Lord to be pleased with my works. I wanted more for me. I needed my purpose to be born. What I had given up on would forever be changed.

Me, yes, my whole perspective on my current situation was evaluated. I was ready. I was willing. Willing to do my work as Iyanla Vanzant with her 'bad' self would say.

I've always had passion for helping others. Most of my career was providing services to young adults. It's a feeling of purpose. It was my love of taking care of them that blessed my soul and the Lord. I want this write to having meaning to many that through Christ one can fail, fall and forgive. Only if we let Him direct our paths. Each morning new grace and mercy is afforded to each one of us. Utilize the Lord, His love and purpose for our lives. He will get the Glory Resulting in our PEACE. Blessings to you all. Amen.

EPILOGUE

Sometimes it's difficult to put your heart's feelings into words. I know the sincerity behind my actions. Its legitimacy has whole heartedly made this writing amazingly easy. After experiencing many years of hurt, the Lord and his vision for me became all I could see. It's called "TESTIMONY." It is the truth I had to live, endure, walk, become and grow through. God wanted me to tell it! When the holy spirit paid me a visit on April 1st, 2017 in my bathroom as I was being purged, he gave me instruction. He clearly said "Share your truths as they will be a blessing to someone." I knew the seed had been planted. It was my job to water it and watch it grow. No one will lose, and a many will gain.

I struggled for many years in my truths. Hurt and fear consumed me. Being sworn to secrecy as a result of someone else's lies wore me out! Hostage I was kept. The neglects of love and compassion in my day to day life was unbearable. Now, learning that you must first love yourself in order to give love to others. The Lord spoke this to me ever so quietly on the night he purged me of all that he wanted me to be rid of. Then he filled me with anew. His AGAPE love overflowed in me. It filled me up to the capacity of my drowning experience. Only God can carry such. Simply because he is so gracious. He returned and rebuilt in me all that was being held hostage. That unconditional Philia love. A love that we as human should always give to one another. This is required of us. Loving is of well doing. My prayer is that I never lose sight again.

Scripture tells us "Let us not become weary in doing good, for at the proper time we will reap a harvest if we do not give up." Galatians 6:9

The experience I had of meeting my Lord and Savior was truly a gift. The sweetness of his presence was most humbling. Never to diminish the reading of the word, simply to magnify the presence of god and his presence. I was in my upper room experience. One, I will forever hold dear to me. God gave me instructions on this day as well. I know these instructions are for the purpose of my continued growth. You see, the Lord not only gives us what we want. When we walk with the Lord, our will aligns with God's will. Micah 6:8. He has made it clear, what is good and required of us. To act with justice, to treasure the Lord's gracious love and to walk humbly in his company.

I then had to take those instructions and apply them to my life. First, ridding myself of what was hindering me most, Me. I was at my lowest when I gave completely up on the desire to love myself. My marriage had fallen into the depths of hell at this point. It was unhealthy and my husband and I were very unhappy. The word clearly tells us, "What therefore God has joined together, let no man put asunder." Mark 10:9. This is nothing shy of the truth. We were out of God's will and in need of working on ourselves to begin the healing process. Clearly this writing is not about the love I have for my husband nor to discredit him in any fashion. Truth be told, we shared a many good times. The day I left my intentions were for my healing to begin. If I had stayed one more day, I truly believe someone would have been preparing my funeral arraignments. The Lord had sent the boat, the water and the life wrath to pull me out of my drowning, and I certainly was not gonna let that ship pass me by.

So here I am today. A work in progress. Walking by faith and not by sight nor my will. Prayerfully staying in the Lord's will. I take life one day at a time. With God's AGAPE love leading the way, I pray continually. I study the word and meditate as this keeps me focused and lined up. This is the dominion I have over my life. I've learned that all that comes and goes in life should not hold so much weight as people, places and things will be in and out of life's seasons. The significance of my growth and prosperity lies in Christ Jesus as He is the author and the finisher of my walk, will, faith and life.

PEACE and love to all.

www.ingramcontent.com/pod-product-compliance
Lightning Source LLC
Chambersburg PA
CBHW071152090426
42736CB00012B/2310